Crikey I'm...

50

Other titles in the *Crikey I'm...* **series**

Crikey I'm A Teenager

Crikey I'm Thirty

Crikey I'm Forty

Crikey I'm Retired

Crikey I'm In Love

Crikey I'm Getting Married

Crikey I'm A Mum

Crikey I'm A Dad

Crikey I'm A Grandparent

Crikey I'm...™

50

Contributors

Dr David Haslam
Victoria Warner
Eliza Williams

Edited by

Steve Hare

Cover Illustration by

Ian Pollock

PURPLE HOUSE

Published by Purple House Limited 1998
75 Banbury Road
Oxford OX2 6PE

© Purple House Limited 1998

Cover illustration: © Ian Pollock/The Inkshed

Crikey I'm... is a trademark of Purple House
Limited

A catalogue record for this book is available
from the British Library

ISBN 1-84118-014-9

Printed in Great Britain by
Cox and Wyman

Acknowledgements

We are grateful to everyone who helped in the compilation of this book, particularly to the following:

Stephen Franks of Franks and Franks (Design)

Inform Group Worldwide (Reproduction)

Dave Kent of the Kobal Collection

Office of National Statistics

Bodleian Library, Oxford

Central Library, Oxford

British Film Institute

Liz Brown

Mark McClintock

Hannah Wren

Illustrations

The Wild One   **3**
A 1955 Pye advertisement   **6**
A National Registration Identity Card   **8**
A 1948 advertisement for Hovis   **12**
The 1951 cast of *The Archers*   **14**
J. Sainsbury's first self-service store   **16**
This is Tomorrow   **19**
Catch-22   **22**
The Post Office Tower   **26**
The Body Shop, 1976   **29**
Adam Faith   **34**
The Swinging Blue Jeans   **37**
The first series of *Blue Peter*   **38**
The Appleyards   **41**
Psycho   **44**
Manfred Mann   **47**
A 1949 Guinness advertisement   **51**

Contents

Crikey I'm 50! 1

Famous Contemporaries 4

Are You a Reincarnation of...? 5

Fifty Not Out 7

What Happened When 17

Fifty FA Cup Winners 32

The Middle Ages 35

Do You Remember...? 39

Can You Imagine Life Without...? 42

Fit at Fifty 45

Fifty Eurovision Winners 52

Top Fifty 54

Crikey, I'm 50!

Somehow, reaching 50 is not the dreaded event that turning 30 and 40 seemed to be at the time. Maybe you're just used to it by now. Maybe you're just too mature to be bothered with such trivial notions. Maybe your friends and acquaintances these days have only ever known you as a distinguished adult.

But 50 is an achievement: half a century; half of the twentieth century. You've been around. You've lasted.

The temptation, then, might be to relax, let it all hang out, or at least down.

Accept that you've lost those youthful looks, and no longer care if you look ridiculous in shorts, or if you can no longer see below your waist as you walk.

But hang about now! Statistically a good percentage of 50 year-olds are barely half way through their lives. You're only just entering middle age. It isn't anything like all over yet.

There's places to go, things to see, try, and do. For many, the children will be growing up and moving out now. Holidays suddenly become cheaper and easier to organise.

And some of those ambitions you almost gave up on long ago – like having a two-seater car, taking up hang-gliding or seeing the world – are practical options once again.

So, after all, perhaps you should be saying to hell with it: I'm going to live for myself now.

This books aims to help you in your resolution to make a new start: to welcome the future with open arms, whilst still celebrating the past 50 full years you've experienced.

Marlon Brando looking moody in *The Wild One*, 1953.

Famous Contemporaries

Paul Smith, fashion designer, born 5/7/46
Bill Clinton, US President, born 19/8/46
Oliver Stone, film director, born 15/9/46
David Bowie, musician, born 8/1/47
Salman Rushdie, author, born 19/6/47
Billy Crystal, actor and comedian, born 14/3/47
Alan Sugar, businessman, born 24/3/47
Jonathan Pryce, actor, born 1/6/47
Kevin Kline, actor, born 24/10/47
Hillary Clinton, First Lady, born 26/10/47
David Mamet, playwright, born 30/11/47
Steven Spielberg, film director, born 18/12/47
Mikhail Baryshnikov, ballet dancer, 27/1/48
Alice Cooper, musician, born 4/2/48
Virginia Bottomley, MP, born 12/3/48
Andrew Lloyd Webber, composer, born 22/3/48
Bob Champion, former jockey, born 4/6/48
Jeremy Irons, actor, born 19/9/48
Stephen King, author, born 21/9/48
Lulu, singer, born 3/11/48
Prince Charles, born 14/11/48
Gérard Depardieu, actor, born 27/12/48
Simon Callow, actor, born 15/6/49
Meryl Streep, actor, born 22/6/49
Martin Amis, author, born 25/8/49
Richard Gere, actor, born 31/8/49
Bruce Springsteen, musician, born 23/9/49
Princess Anne, born 15/8/50
Suzi Quatro, musician, born 3/6/50
Richard Branson, entrepreneur, born 18/7/50
Kevin Keegan, footballer/commentator, born 14/2/51
John Goodman, actor, born 20/6/52
Jeff Goldblum, actor, born 22/10/52
Imran Khan, cricketer and politician, born 25/11/52
Clive Anderson, television presenter, born 10/12/52

Are You a Reincarnation of...?

Mohandas Karamchand 'Mahatma' Gandhi, Indian statesman, died 30/1/48

Orville Wright, US aviation pioneer, died 30/1/48

Sergei Eisenstein, film director, died 11/2/48

George Herman 'Babe' Ruth, baseball player, died 16/8/48

Mohammed Ali Jinnah, first Governor-General of Pakistan, died 11/9/48

Margaret Mitchell, author, died 16/8/49

Richard Strauss, composer, died 8/9/49

George Orwell, author, died 21/1/50

Edgar Rice Burroughs, author, died 19/3/50

Kurt Weill, composer, died 3/4/50

Al Jolson, singer and actor, died 23/10/50

George Bernard Shaw, author, died 2/10/50

Max Beckmann, painter, died 27/12/50

Ivor Novello, composer and actor, 6/3/51

Ludwig Wittgenstein, philosopher, died 29/4/51

Willliam Kellogg, cereal tycoon, died 6/10/51

King George VI, died 6/2/52

Albert Einstein, scientist, died 13/2/52

Maria Montessori, educationalist, died 6/5/52

Eva Peron, 'Evita', politician, died 26/7/52

Dr Chaim Weizmann, first President of Israel, 9/11/52

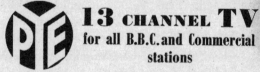

13 CHANNEL TV
for all B.B.C. and Commercial stations

High technology from Pye in 1955.

Fifty Not Out

A Look At The World Fifty Years Ago

The world into which you were born at the end of the forties and early fifties is a strange and distant place, as remote as history, laughably quaint. Memories and impressions – based largely on film footage and family photographs – are inevitably in black and white, and slightly stilted. The soundtrack of your earliest years is punctuated by clipped, artificial accents. Heavy and brittle records spun at 78rpm. BBC radio offered the staid delights of the Light Programme or the Home Service, and the Third Programme, started in 1946.

At the age of 50, you will have grown an average of 18.7 metres of finger nails.

Television then was an almost unimaginable luxury, something utterly remarkable, like a car that wasn't black, a ball-point pen, or a shop laden with fresh oranges, bananas and pineapples. In 1948 a person's weekly rations were lower even than in wartime: one ounce of cooking fat, one egg, one and a half ounces of cheese, two pints of milk. And, never even contemplated during the War, bread was rationed until 1948. Almost inedible snoek and whalemeat were sold instead of cod and haddock. Coal, petrol, sheets and clothes were all in desperately short supply; whisky was almost unobtainable.

NATIONAL
REGISTRATION

IDENTITY
CARD

UNDER SIXTEEN YEARS

During and after World War 2, all children were issued with identity cards until 1952.

It was a wrecked world, every major British city ravaged by bombing raids, littered with derelict sites. Damaged houses could not be repaired fast enough, nor prefabs and permanent homes erected in sufficient numbers to meet the urgent needs of homeless families, many of whom squatted in wartime camps and empty blocks of flats, often organised and supervised by an active Communist Party.

1947 had started with the worst winter this century, bringing the country to a standstill, with power stations closing for lack of fuel. Root vegetables had to be dug up with drills and pickaxes, and thousands of farm animals lay dead beneath immense snow-drifts. Ice floes were seen in the North Sea. Rivers froze, only to burst their banks in floods a month or so later.

And yet: there was a sense of optimism in the air, as hastily married couples finally found the time to get to know each other, and millions turned in their uniforms for demob suits. The new Labour government had been returned by a landslide, with the avowed aim of making the country a more equitable place, nationalising the railways and mines. And in 1948 they were able to realise the main promise on which they had swept to victory: introducing the National Health Service, despite the

50 year-olds watch an average of 26 hours of television per week.

hostility of the BMA, who were accused by Aneurin 'Nye' Bevan of 'organised sabotage'. Within its first year, more than five million NHS pairs of glasses were dispensed, and many more dental patients treated, free of charge.

> 'Everything got better after I was 50. I wrote my best books. I walked Pillar, starting from Buttermere, which I'm told no fell walker of advanced years should attempt'
>
> A. J. P. Taylor, interviewed in *The Evening Standard*, March 1982

The optimism was officially sponsored: first through the 'Britain Can Make It' exhibition in 1946 – held in the still-empty Victoria and Albert Museum, its contents evacuated for safety to the country. And later, the Festival of Britain in 1951; attended, and fondly remembered by more than eight million people.

But nationalisation alone was no cure for Britain's huge debt, the shortage of housing, food, raw materials and the slow pace of reconstruction.

The Festival was prepared and planned against a sea of antipathy, predominantly from the Conservative opposition and the right-wing press, both using arguments curiously reminiscent of recent coverage of the Millennium Dome.

Construction at the Festival site was delayed by the inevitable shortages of materials and labour. Meanwhile, Labour's majority in Parliament was whittled away. Bevan and Harold Wilson resigned over proposals to charge for false teeth and glasses. But the Festival attracted happy millions, gazing in wonder at the Dome of Discovery and the Skylon tower.

And at the end of the Festival, with Labour back in opposition, one of the first acts of the new administration was to raze the entire site, despite the fact that the major structures were all designed to be dismantled and re-erected elsewhere, and despite the fact that there were substantial cash offers for them. The South Bank site was to remain derelict for more than a decade, when an office block and car park erased any lingering memories.

Internationally, reconstruction and social change gathered pace. After a long and unrelenting guerrilla campaign, Mao Tse-tung was proclaimed Chairman of a Communist China in 1949. Russian influence began to extend into Eastern Europe, and North Korea. The British Empire was in the process of dismantling itself: India, Ceylon, Burma all gained independence; likewise Cambodia gained independence from France.

The breadwinner eats

more Hovis now . . .

to keep up his strength

the sensible way

Hovis THE BETTER-BALANCED BREAD

Hovis targets hard workers in 1948.

By the age of 50, you will have worked continuously for an average of 5.4 years.

The world, still weary from six years' fighting and destruction, would soon see renewed conflict in Korea, the first major test between American and communist ideology.

The technology of World War II, Spitfires and Lancaster bombers, had already been replaced by jet aircraft.

The first computers, transistors and artificial hearts were built.

Nuclear reactors started up and, despite the objections of Albert Einstein, the testing of nuclear devices continued at Bikini Atoll and Siberia as Russia and the USA vied to realign the balance of power, under the umbrella of a growing mushroom cloud.

Elsewhere in Europe and around the world, millions of 'displaced persons' and refugees sought out their families and a new home. Many had no home or family left: some had no country.

'Fifty today, old lad? Well, that's not doing so bad.'

Kingsley Amis

Yugoslavia was reeling from civil war, partition and annexation, and the ravages of the Ustachi.

The faces behind the voices: the cast of *The Archers* in 1951.

Violence continued in Palestine between Arab and Jew; between Muslim and Hindu in India. Argentina's campaign to regain the Falkland Islands was renewed. South African Nationalists began the systematic introduction of apartheid.

Such was the peace, 50 years ago.

By the age of 50, you will have produced an average of 27,000 litres of urine.

J. Sainsbury's first self-service store opens in Croydon in 1950.

What Happened When

A Brief Review of the Last Fifty Years

1950
- India is proclaimed a republic.
- Senator McCarthy launches an anti-communist crusade in the US.

1951
- The first hydrogen bomb is tested by the US on Eniwetok Atoll in the mid Pacific.

1952
- King George VI dies in his sleep and Princess Elizabeth is pronounced Queen at the age of 25.
- An artificial heart is transplanted successfully for the first time in Philadelphia, US.
- *The New Musical Express* publishes Britain's first pop chart.

1953
- Edmund Hillary and Sherpa Tenzing are the first to climb to the summit of Mount Everest.
- Queen Elizabeth's Coronation is televised live.

1954
- A link between smoking and lung cancer is established.
- Roger Bannister, aged 25, breaks the four-minute mile.
- Rationing ends in Britain after 14 years.

1955

• Commercial television begins in the UK. BBC radio grabs a major audience on the night by killing off Grace Archer in *The Archers*.

• *Lolita* by Vladimir Nabokov is published.

1956

• Elvis performs on *The Ed Sullivan Show* to a huge TV audience in the US.

• The film *Rock Around the Clock* causes riots in cinemas across the UK.

1957

• The Russians launch the first man-made satellite, Sputnik-1.

1958

• Eight Manchester United players, the 'Busby Babes', are killed in an aircrash in Munich.

• The drug Thalidomide, prescribed for morning sickness in pregnancy, is found to cause birth defects.

1959

• Fidel Castro wrests power in Cuba from the dictator Batista.

• The first Mini, capable of 70 mph, is on the road.

1960s

1960

• The trial of the publication of *Lady Chatterley's Lover* begins in London. Publication is allowed and the first 200,000 copies sell out in a day.

this is tomorrow whitechapel art gallery

aug. 9 - sept 9 1956

The exhibition *This is Tomorrow*, including works by Richard Hamilton and Eduardo Paolozzi, is credited with launching the Pop Art movement in 1956.

- John F. Kennedy becomes the US president.
- *Coronation Street* is first broadcast by Granada.

1961

- The oral contraceptive pill becomes available in the UK.
- The Russians launch a man, Yuri Gagarin, into space for the first time for 108 minutes in the Vostok spacecraft.
- The East/West German border is closed and the Berlin Wall is erected.

1962

- Marilyn Monroe is found dead in an apparent suicide.
- The Telstar communications satellite transmits the first live transatlantic television.

1963

- £2.6 million is stolen in the Great Train Robbery.
- Kennedy is assassinated in Dallas allegedly by Lee Harvey Oswald.
- Beatlemania grips Britain.

1964

- Cassius Clay becomes the heavyweight world champion.
- There are clashes between Mods and Rockers in coastal towns in Britain.
- Nelson Mandela is sentenced to life imprisonment in South Africa for 'treason'.
- America goes to war against the North Vietnamese communists.
- *Top of the Pops* begins broadcasting on BBC.

1965

- Ian Brady and Myra Hindley are arrested for the murder of Lesley Ann Downing and the police search for more bodies.
- The death penalty is abolished in Britain.

1966

- London is officially 'swinging'.
- England win the World Cup, beating Germany 4–2.
- Chairman Mao announces a cultural revolution in China.
- A slag heap in Aberfan, South Wales, collapses and buries the local school, killing 116 children and 28 adults.
- The introduction of pantyhose (or tights) across the world.

1967

- Protests against the war in Vietnam occur in the US and in Europe.
- Israel defeats the Arabs in the Six-Day War.
- It is 'the summer of love', with hippie music festivals, psychedelic drugs and flower-power.
- BBC 2 makes the first European colour broadcasts.
- BBC radio drops the Light and Third Programmes and the Home Service in favour of stations 1, 2, 3 and 4.
- The first human heart transplant is performed by Dr Christiaan Barnard.
- The Abortion Act legalises abortion in Britain.

1968

- Martin Luther King is shot dead in Memphis.
- Republican Richard Nixon becomes the US president.
- 13 members of the cast of *Hair* appear naked on stage after play censorship is lifted.

Joseph Heller's *Catch-22*, first published in 1961.

1969

• A human egg is fertilised in a test tube for the first time in Britain.

• US astronauts, Neil Armstrong and Edwin 'Buzz' Aldrin land on the moon.

• Half a million people attend the first free rock festival, held for three days in Woodstock, US.

• Sharon Tate and four others are murdered by Charles Manson's cult 'family'.

1970s

1970

• Strikes by dockers, national newspapers, and local authorities throughout the year in Britain.

• The age of majority is reduced in Britain from 21 to 18.

• Schools in Britain switch from a selective to a comprehensive system.

• The Gay Liberation Front is formed.

1971

• The first British soldier is killed in Ulster since troops entered in 1969.

• Decimal currency is introduced in Britain.

1972

• British troops kill 13 in Londonderry's 'Bloody Sunday' after a civil rights march turns into a riot.

• Miners' strikes over pay claims cause blackouts across Britain. Householders are asked to only heat one room and industry is officially working a three-day week.

- Nixon aides are arrested for trying to bug the Democrat headquarters in the Watergate complex. Nixon denies any responsibility and is re-elected.
- The Race Relations Act comes into force in Britain.

1973

- Britain officially joins the EEC.
- 'Glam Rock', featuring artists such as Gary Glitter, T-Rex and Elton John, is popular.

1974

- Nixon resigns after admitting to participation in the Watergate scandal. He is the first US President to resign.
- Lord Lucan disappears after allegedly murdering his nanny and attacking his estranged wife.

1975

- The war in Vietnam is over as Saigon is taken by the North Vietnamese and all US troops are withdrawn.
- Bill Gates, aged 19, and a friend, form the Microsoft computer company.
- *Jaws* (directed by Steven Spielberg) is released.

1976

- A boiling British summer leads to the instigation of the Droughts Bill to tackle water shortages.

1977

- 25 years of the Queen's reign are celebrated by a week of Silver Jubilee celebrations in the summer.
- Elvis Presley dies in a suspected drug-related death at his

mansion, Graceland.

• Two homosexual men die and are thought to be the first AIDS (Acquired Immune Deficiency Syndrome) victims in New York.

• Punk music is prominent and projects The Sex Pistols, The Clash, The Jam and Iggy Pop to fame.

1978

• Sid Vicious is charged with murdering his girlfriend Nancy Spungen.

1979

• Vietnamese forces seize control of Cambodia, overthrowing the Khmer Rouge. Pol Pot's killing fields are discovered.

• Margaret Thatcher becomes the first female British Prime Minister.

• Sebastian Coe breaks world records in the 800 metres, 1,500 metres and the mile.

1980s

1980

• John Lennon is shot dead outside his apartment building in New York.

• Rubik's Cube mania sweeps the country.

1981

• 'Yorkshire Ripper' Peter Sutcliffe is arrested for the murder of 13 women.

• Prince Charles and Lady Diana Spencer marry.

• Republican Ronald Reagan becomes US President.

The Post Office Tower, London, opens in 1965.

1982

- The first test tube twins are born in Britain.
- Argentina invades and captures the Falkland Islands but is defeated by the British troops after a two-month war.
- Channel 4 goes on air in Britain. The first programme is the quiz show *Countdown*.

1983

- The pound coin comes into circulation.

1984

- Concern grows over the 'greenhouse effect'.
- A nationwide miners' strike follows pit closures.
- An IRA bomb blasts the Tory conference HQ in Brighton killing four, but narrowly missing Margaret Thatcher.
- Band Aid release *Do They Know It's Christmas* to raise money for famine victims in Africa.

1985

- Bob Geldof organises the 'Live Aid' concert for aid to Africa at Wembley Stadium and raises £50 million.

1986

- The American space shuttle Challenger explodes seconds after take-off, killing all on board.
- Radiation is released during a fire at Chernobyl nuclear reactor in Russia.
- The M25 is officially opened by Margaret Thatcher.

1987

- Terry Waite is held hostage in Lebanon.

- 187 die as *The Herald of Free Enterprise* ferry sinks leaving Zeebrugge.
- Michael Ryan shoots 16 dead in Hungerford and then shoots himself.
- The stock market falls by 10% on 'Black Monday', causing the worst crash this century.
- The worst storm this century in England kills 18 people.
- 30 die in a fire at King's Cross tube station.
- Reagan and Gorbachev sign a mutual agreement to cut the size of their nuclear arsenals.

1988
- Soviet Perestroika goes into effect.
- Edwina Currie causes a political storm over announcements over salmonella in eggs. She is forced to resign.
- Pan Am flight 103 from London to New York crashes in Lockerbie, Scotland, killing all aboard.

1989
- Salman Rushdie is condemned to death for blasphemy following the publication of *The Satanic Verses*.
- 94 fans die in the Hillsborough stadium disaster in Sheffield.
- Tanks roll into Tiananmen Square in China and crush democracy attempts, killing more than 2,000 people.
- 'The Guildford Four' are released from jail after 14 years.
- The Berlin Wall is pulled down, symbolising the end of Soviet international communism.
- Ceausescu, the Romanian dictator, and his wife, are executed after being found guilty for attempting to crush demonstrations against the communist government.

The first Body Shop opens in 1976.

1990

• The government gives £2.2 million for research into BSE, known as 'mad cow disease'.

• Authorities in South Africa lift the 30-year ban on the ANC (African National Congress) and Nelson Mandela is released from jail.

• Demonstrations against the Poll Tax take place across Britain.

• East and West Germany are reunified.

• Thatcher resigns as British PM to be replaced by John Major.

1991

• The Gulf War begins after Iraqi troops refuse to withdraw from Kuwait by the deadline given by the UN.

• The 'Birmingham Six' are released.

• Apartheid collapses in South Africa.

• Civil war breaks out in Yugoslavia between Serbs, Croats and Muslims.

• Robert Maxwell is found drowned after vanishing from his yacht.

• Terry Waite, the last British hostage, is freed after being held in Beirut for five years.

1992

• Mike Tyson is sent to jail for six months for raping Miss Black America contestant, Desiree Washington.

1993

• Two ten year-old boys are arrested and found guilty of the

murder of toddler James Bulger.
- The European Union is formed with the implementation of the Maastricht treaty.

1994
- The Church of England decides to ordain seven women priests.
- Frederick and Rosemary West are charged with the murder of eight women found in the garden of their house.
- Following the sudden death of John Smith, Tony Blair becomes the leader of the Labour party.
- The Channel Tunnel opens between Britain and France.
- Nelson Mandela is inaugurated as South Africa's first black President.
- £7 million is spent on the first day of UK Lottery sales.
- The rise of 'drum 'n' bass' in Britain.

1995
- Nick Leeson, 28, is arrested in Germany for causing the collapse of Barings Bank by gambling on high risk derivatives on the Singapore market.
- Damien Hirst receives the Turner Prize for *Mother and Child Divided*, a bisected cow and calf, which causes demonstrations by animal rights protesters.
- The rise of 'Brit Pop' with chart wars between Blur, Oasis, Pulp, Supergrass...

Fifty FA Cup Winners

1998 Arsenal 2 Newcastle 0

1997 Chelsea 2 Middlesborough 0

1996 Manchester United 1 Liverpool 0

1995 Everton 1 Manchester United 0

1994 Manchester United 4 Chelsea 0

1993 Arsenal 1:2 Sheffield Wednesday 1:1*

1992 Liverpool 2 Sunderland 0

1991 Tottenham Hotspur 2 Nottingham Forest 1*

1990 Manchester United 3:1 Crystal Palace 3:0

1989 Liverpool 3 Everton 2*

1988 Wimbledon 1 Liverpool 0

1987 Coventry City 3 Tottenham Hotspur 2*

1986 Liverpool 3 Everton 1

1985 Manchester United 1 Everton 0*

1984 Everton 2 Watford 0

1983 Manchester United 2:4 Brighton & Hove Albion 2:0

1982 Tottenham Hotspur 1:1 Queen's Park Rangers 1:0

1981 Tottenham Hotspur 1:3 Manchester City 1:2

1980 West Ham United 1 Arsenal 0

1979 Arsenal 3 Manchester United 2

1978 Ipswich Town 1 Arsenal 0

1977 Manchester United 2 Liverpool 1

1976 Southampton 1 Manchester United 0

1975 West Ham United 2 Fulham 0

1974 Liverpool 3 Newcastle United 0

1973 Sunderland 1 Leeds United 0

1972 Leeds United 1 Arsenal 0

1971 Arsenal 2 Liverpool 1

1970 Chelsea 2:2 Leeds United 2:1*

1969 Manchester City 1 Leicester City 0

1968 West Bromwich Albion 1 Everton 0*

1967 Tottenham Hotspur 2 Chelsea 1

1966 Everton 3 Sheffield Wednesday 2

1965 Liverpool 2 Leeds United 1*

1964 West Ham United 3 Preston North End 2

1963 Manchester United 3 Leicester City 1

1962 Tottenham Hotspur 3 Burnley 1

1961 Tottenham Hotspur 2 Leicester City 0

1960 Wolverhampton Wanderers 3 Blackburn Rovers 0

1959 Nottingham Forest 2 Luton Town 1

1958 Bolton Wanderers 2 Manchester United 0

1957 Aston Villa 2 Manchester United 1

1956 Manchester City 3 Birmingham City 1

1955 Newcastle United 3 Manchester City 1

1954 West Bromwich Albion 3 Preston North End 2

1953 Blackpool 4 Bolton Wanderers 3

1952 Newcastle United 1 Arsenal 0

1951 Newcastle United 2 Blackpool 0

1950 Arsenal 2 Liverpool 0

1949 Wolverhampton Wanderers 3 Leicester City 1

(*indicates extra time)

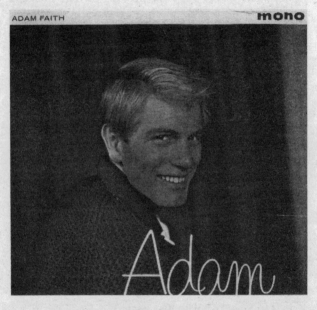

Adam Faith's album *Adam* charms teenage girls in 1960.

The Middle Ages

Fifty Then And Now

Fifty isn't, by any means, old. These days, some women are even having children at this age. At this time, your career may be peaking, while financial security becomes more assured and the mortgage might even be paid off. If you have children, they are probably older and maybe even self-sufficient now, leaving many people with more time and money to do the things they always wanted to.

By 50, you will have blinked an average of 276 million times.

Pity, then, 50 year-olds in centuries gone by. Primarily, of course, you'd have been lucky to reach 50 at all in the seventeenth century: statistically, you'd be long gone. The average life expectancy back then hovered at around 20 years, which would make you well and truly ancient. Only five per cent of the population made it to 60, and the chances of getting past 50 weren't much better.

The body seemed to age much more quickly back then – probably owing to poor nutrition for the majority of people – and you would certainly have looked older than your 50 years. You were also much more prone to illness – and in the seventeenth, eighteenth, and even as recently as last century, there were plenty around. Epidemics of smallpox and cholera in the eighteenth and nineteenth centuries would have hit the old and the young particularly hard. It wasn't all bad news for 50 year-olds, though: many people thought that older individuals were less susceptible to bubonic plague.

As poor health was increasingly likely beyond the age of 40, you might have found it difficult to work. Your family may have been able to shelter you; but if they were equally poorly-off, you'd probably have been thrown on the mercy of the parish or the workhouse. Unless you had sufficient means to maintain yourself without work, you may well have been destitute by the age of 50.

On an average week a 50 year-old spends 59 hours asleep; 40 hours on free time; 26 hours in paid work; 24 hours in domestic work; 14 hours in personal care and 6 hours on household maintenance. They have an average of 5 hours' free time on a weekday and 7 hours of free time on a weekend day.

Things have changed rather a lot since those dark days. The good news for British 50 year-olds is that there are more of you in this country, proportionately speaking, than in any other country in the world. Spare a thought for the residents of Uganda, Malawi, Niger, Guinea, Rwanda and Madagascar, however; only 16 per cent of their populations live past the age of 50. Medical advances in the West mean that most of its inhabitants, by contrast, will live to their mid seventies at least. Plenty of time yet, then, to finish that decorating you've been putting off for so long!

The Swinging Blue Jeans rock the kids in 1964.

Christopher Trace and Leila Williams present the first series of *Blue Peter* in 1958.

Do You Remember...?

Blasts From The Past

Children's TV from the 1950s

The Appleyards
Playbox
Picture Book
Zoo Quest – David Attenborough.
Watch With Mother – with Andy Pandy (and Looby Loo and Teddy), *The Woodentops*, and *Bill and Ben*.
Hopalong Cassidy
Champion the Wonder Horse
The Lone Ranger
The Range Rider
Hot Chestnut Man – with Johnny Morris.
Picture Book
Captain Pugwash
Blue Peter – the first puppy died after its initial appearance on the show in 1962 and, unknown to viewers, was replaced by a lookalike and later named Petra. Other canine stars include Bonnie, Honey, Patch, Goldie and Shep (hence John Noakes' well-known byline 'Get down, Shep').
Muffin the Mule

> Here comes Muffin the mule, Muffin the mule,
> Dear old Muffin, playing the fool.
> Here comes Muffin, everybody sing
> Here comes Muffin the mule.

Popular songs from the early 1960s

Adam Faith – *What Do You Want* reached No. 1 in 1959, *Lonely Pup (In A Christmas Shop)* reached No. 4 in 1960.
Craig Douglas – *Only Sixteen* reached No. 1 in 1959.
Cliff Richard – *Living Doll* reached No. 1 in 1959, *Please Don't Tease* reached No. 1 in 1960, *The Young Ones* reached No. 1 in 1962.
The Everly Brothers – *Cathy's Clown* reached No. 1 in 1960, *Walk Right Back* reached No. 1 in 1961.
The Shadows – *Apache* reached No. 1 in 1960, *Kon-Tiki* reached No. 1 in 1961, *Wonderful Land* reached No. 1 in 1962.

Helen Shapiro – *You Don't Know* and *Walkin' Back To Happiness* reached No. 1 in 1961.

Elvis Presley – *Are You Lonesome Tonight* reached No. 1 in 1961, *Can't Help Falling In Love* reached No. 1 in 1962, *You're the Devil in Disguise* reached No. 1 in 1963.

Dave Brubeck Quartet – *Take Five* reached No. 6 in 1961.

Petula Clark – *Sailor* reached No. 1 in 1961.

Chubby Checker – *Let's Twist Again* reached No. 2 in 1961.

Eden Kane – *Well I Ask You* reached No. 1 in 1961.

Billy Fury – *Jealousy* reached No. 2 in 1961.

Mike Sarne (with Wendy Richard) – *Come Outside* reached No. 1 in 1962.

Brenda Lee – *Speak To Me Pretty* reached No. 3 in 1962.

Frank Ifield – *I Remember You* and *Lovesick Blues* reached No. 1 in 1962, *Confessin'* reached No. 1 in 1963.

Ray Charles – *I Can't Stop Loving You* reached No. 1 in 1962.

The Searchers – *Sweets For My Sweet* reached No. 1 in 1963.

The Beatles – *From Me To You, She Loves You, I Want To Hold Your Hand* all reached No. 1 in 1963.

Swinging Blue Jeans – *Hippy Hippy Shake* reached No. 2 in 1963.

Popular Dances

Bossa Nova

Shake

Beeje

Twist – In 1962, an Essex schoolboy claimed to have danced the Twist non-stop for 33 hours, breaking the world record.

Mashed Potato

Locomotion

Hully Gully

The Hula-Hoop

The cast of *The Appleyards* in 1955.

Can You Imagine Life Without...

Popular Inventions In Your Lifetime

Tupperware – Made by Earl Tupper in 1939 after he had purified left-over synthetic material. In 1947, he began making food storage containers and selling them to stores; in 1949, he was recommended by Brownie Wise to sell them at 'parties'. He became a millionaire.

Liquid Paper (otherwise known as Tipp-ex) – Betty Nesmith created Liquid Paper after beginning a new job in 1951 and being nervous of making typing mistakes. She took some white tempera waterbase paint to work with her in a nail-polish bottle. It finally took off in 1958 after her friends spread the word and the product was mentioned in *Office* magazine. In 1979, Gillette paid $48 million for the product. She was also the mother of Mike Nesmith from The Monkees.

Cat Litter – Designed in 1947 by Edward Lowe after a customer's cat sandbox froze solid. She wanted sawdust, but Lowe suggested kiln-dried granulated clay, as it was less of a fire hazard.

Velcro – Patented in 1951 by Swiss engineer George de Mestral, it didn't make its debut on the market until the early sixties.

Bic pens – Marcel Bich produced the first Bic ballpoint in 1949. The first ballpoint pens were introduced in 1945, but they were messy and had to be held perpendicular to the paper for the ink to flow properly. They were also very expensive. Bich solved all these problems and his plastic ballpoints became available very cheaply.

Compact Discs – In 1982, the first CDs and players were launched by Philips. Initially only 150 music titles were made. However, due to popular demand by both buyers and artists, it is now the most common form of music media.

Calculator – The first electronic calculator was made in 1946 in the US. It filled several large rooms and contained over 18,000 valves. By 1971 an electronic circuit had been made that was small enough to create pocket-sized calculators.

Rubber Gloves – First invented in 1952 for surgical and industrial use. The London Rubber Company launched the household rubber glove in 1961.

Computer – The idea of the first mechanical computer was conceived by Charles Babbage in 1835, but never went beyond the design stage. The first computer was built by Americans John Mauchley and John Eckert in 1946, and weighed 30 tons. The first word processor was devised by the IBM company in 1964, but was the size of a desk and had no screen.

Janet Leigh in Alfred Hitchcock's *Psycho*, 1960.

Fit At Fifty

Dr David Haslam

When you were a teenager, did you ever imagine that you would be 50? The Who were singing 'hope I die before I get old', and preached that you should never trust anyone over 30. In those days, 50 seemed unbelievably old, but now you've got here you still feel youthful, fit, and dynamic. Or at least you do most of the time!

For many people, turning 50 makes them very depressed. They look around at our increasingly youth-dominated culture, and feel left behind. However, whilst 50 year-olds of the past generally looked and behaved like old people, the baby-boomer generation has refused to let its sense of fun and optimism fade away.

For most people who have made it to 50, there will be at least another 25 years of life to live and enjoy. To make the most of this time, you do need to look after yourself, and this chapter will tell you how.

Your Changing Body
When scientists have looked at healthy 80 year-olds – and that is 30 years away for you – it is clear that the seeds of their continuing good health are sown at a much younger age. If you want to keep fit, and to have a long and active life, the rules are simple and certainly shouldn't be too painful.

• Exercise regularly – at least three times a week,

doing exercise that you enjoy, though if this means increasing your exercise dramatically, do check with your doctor first.

- Keep your alcohol intake below an absolute maximum of 28 units a week for men and 21 for women – ideally less.

- Keep your body weight to within 20 per cent of the ideal, and eat three healthy meals a day.

- Get adequate sleep and relaxation.

- Don't smoke. If you are still smoking, it's never too late to stop.

- Both women and men should ensure that their blood pressure is checked at least once a year. Women should be aware of any changes in their breasts, and should ensure that they have regular cervical smear tests, and men should regularly self-examine their testicles. If you don't know how, ask your GP. Men who develop difficulties passing urine should have their prostate gland checked.

- In women, the fifties may be the time when her safe reproductive years will be coming to an end, and the menopause starts, if it hasn't already. Typical signs are hot flushes, mood swings, vaginal dryness, and erratic periods. But despite all the stories and articles, for one third of women the menopause causes no problems at all; for one third it can be a nuisance; and for one third it causes significant symptoms. Problems are not inevitable.

The five faces of Manfred Mann – Mike Hugg, Paul Jones, Manfred Mann, Tom McGuiness and Mike Vickers in 1964.

- For women, osteoporosis can start to be a significant problem after the age of 50. It does tend to run in families, but can be aggravated by a poor diet, smoking, and lack of exercise. All of these are factors that you can influence, and in addition, hormone replacement therapy can act as a prevention. If you are concerned, do talk to your GP or practice nurse.

For many people in their fifties, every twinge of pain feels like the start of something dreadful, from cancer to a heart attack. Remember that most people in their fifties are still extremely fit, and that positive thinkers do tend to stay fitter for longer. However, there are two symptoms that you should never ignore:

- Any bleeding from the anus should be assessed by a doctor – don't just blame it on piles.

- You should also take seriously any chest pain that is brought on by exertion and eased by rest.

Your Changing Emotions

If you are in regular employment, and your children are grown-up and financially independent, you may be better off now than you've ever been in your life. And if the mortgage has been paid off, life is even better. So – have fun; spoil yourself if you can. Take those dream holidays: but do make sure that you are saving for an adequate pension.

It may seem early, but start to think about what you are going to do when you retire. You may spend a third of your life in retirement: doing the garden and watching TV probably won't be enough to keep you amused. Think ahead, plan new and different activities for the years ahead, maybe even join a gym. You need only be an inactive old fogey if that's what you want. You are never too old to learn, but lots of people use age as an excuse.

Don't think that the menopause spells the end for sexual desire. Research has shown that for at least eight out of ten women, sexual responsiveness either increases or stays the same after the change. There really is no excuse for your love life to become boring. If you do run into problems, talk to each other and discuss your feelings openly. And don't forget the power of romance. Men who leave their socks on can hardly be surprised if women don't find them erotic!

This is also a great time for strengthening your relationship with your partner generally, as well as sexually. Spend plenty of time together, and make the most of each other's company. Don't take each other for granted. Even after all these years, it is important to show your appreciation for one another.

By now, you may have grandchildren. Once, the popular image of a granny was that of an old lady in a rocking chair. Now modern grannies join, and even run, aerobics classes! Spoil your grandchildren like you didn't spoil your own children. And there's a great advantage – you can hand them back when they start to whine.

However, the 'empty nest syndrome' is distressing for some women, particularly those for whom parenthood, rather than being an independent occupation, defined their view of themselves. This group, perhaps more than any other, needs to take positive steps into new areas of opportunity.

Improvements in health and changing social attitudes now mean that the fifties can be seen as one of the prime times of life, rather than as a steady downhill slope. Indeed, as the baby-boom generation moves through their fifties, and the overall birth-rate declines, there are actually fewer young people. Thus, far from opportunities dwindling as you get older, chances are that the opportunities for older people will be better than in the past.

There has certainly never been a better time throughout history to be 50. Enjoy it.

David Haslam is married with two children and has been a GP for 22 years. He is a Fellow of the Royal College of General Practitioners, and has written numerous books – the most recent being Stress Free Parenting. *He also writes a column for* Practical Parenting *magazine, and frequently broadcasts on health topics*

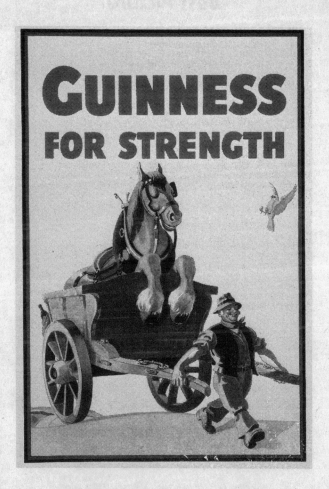

The benefits of drinking Guinness in 1949.

50 Oscar Winners For Best Picture

1997 *Titanic* (dir. James Cameron)

1996 *The English Patient* (dir. Anthony Minghella)

1995 *Braveheart* (dir. Mel Gibson)

1994 *Forrest Gump* (dir. Robert Zemeckis)

1993 *Schindler's List* (dir. Stephen Spielberg)

1992 *Unforgiven* (dir. Clint Eastwood)

1991 *The Silence of the Lambs* (dir. Jonathan Demme)

1990 *Dances With Wolves* (dir. Kevin Costner)

1989 *Driving Miss Daisy* (dir. Bruce Beresford)

1988 *Rain Man* (dir. Barry Levinson)

1987 *The Last Emperor* (dir. Bernardo Bertolucci)

1986 *Platoon* (dir. Oliver Stone)

1985 *Out of Africa* (dir. Sydney Pollack)

1984 *Amadeus* (dir. Milos Forman)

1983 *Terms of Endearment* (dir. James L. Brook)

1982 *Gandhi* (dir. Richard Attenborough)

1981 *Chariots of Fire* (dir. Hugh Hudson)

1980 *Ordinary People* (dir. Robert Redford)

1979 *Kramer vs. Kramer* (dir. Robert Benton)

1978 *The Deer Hunter* (dir. Michael Cimino)

1977 *Annie Hall* (dir. Woody Allen)

1976 *Rocky* (dir. John G. Avildsen)

1975 *One Flew Over the Cuckoo's Nest* (dir. Milos Forman)

1974 *The Godfather Part II* (dir. Francis Ford Coppola)

1973 *The Sting* (dir. George Roy Hill)

1972 *The Godfather* (dir. Francis Ford Coppola)

1971 *The French Connection* (dir. William Friedkin)

1970 *Patton* (dir. Franklin Schaffner)

1969 *Midnight Cowboy* (dir. John Schlesinger)

1968 *Oliver!* (dir. Carol Reed)

1967 *In the Heat of the Night* (dir. Norman Jewison)

1966 *A Man For All Seasons* (dir. Fred Zinnemann)

1965 *The Sound of Music* (dir. Robert Wise)

1964 *My Fair Lady* (dir. George Cukor)

1963 *Tom Jones* (dir. Tony Richardson)

1962 *Lawrence of Arabia* (dir. David Lean)

1961 *West Side Story* (dir. Robert Wise/Jerome Robbins)

1960 *The Apartment* (dir. Billy Wilder)

1959 *Ben-Hur* (dir. Fred Niblo)

1958 *Gigi* (dir. Vincente Minnelli)

1957 *The Bridge on the River Kwai* (dir. David Lean)

1956 *Around the World in 80 Days*

     (dir. Michael Anderson/Kevin McClory)

1955 *Marty* (dir. Delbert Mann)

1954 *On the Waterfront* (dir. Elia Kazan)

1953 *From Here to Eternity* (dir. Fred Zinnemann)

1952 *The Greatest Show on Earth* (dir. Cecil B. de Mille)

1951 *An American in Paris* (dir. Vincente Minelli)

1950 *All About Eve* (dir. Joseph L. Mankiewicz)

1949 *All the King's Men* (dir. Robert Rossen)

1948 *Hamlet* (dir. Laurence Olivier)

Top Fifty

Fame Comes to Those Who Wait

Marx wrote *Das Kapital* aged 49

•

Raymond Chandler published his first novel, *The Big Sleep*, at the age of 51

•

R. G. Adams wrote *Watership Down* aged 52, after a career in the civil service

•

Margaret Thatcher became Prime Minister at 53

•

Mao Tse-tung became head of state for the People's Republic of China at the age of 55

•

Rex Harrison was 56 when he won an Oscar for his role in *My Fair Lady*

•

Mikhail Gorbachev became the Russian leader aged 54

•

George Washington became the first President of the USA at the age of 57

•

Daniel Defoe published *Robinson Crusoe*, his first novel, at the age of 59

•

Darwin published *The Origin of Species* aged 50

•

Wilhelm von Röntgen discovered X-rays in 1901, aged 50

•

William Jenney invented the skyscraper at the age of 52

•

Maurice Ravel composed *Bolero* aged 53

•

Glenda Jackson became Labour MP for Hampstead and Highgate aged 56, following a long acting career

•

William Hartnell was 55 when he first starred in *Dr Who*

•

Terry Venables became the manager of England at the age of 51

•

Martin Bell was 58 when he became MP for Tatton following an extensive journalistic career

Copyright Notices